The IV-C Mercury Tox Program®

A Guide for the Patient

H.L. "Sam" Queen
Betty A. Queen

A publication of
The Institute for Health Realities

The Institute for Health Realities, Inc.
Post Office Box 49308
Colorado Springs, Colorado, 80949-9308

2nd Edition Revised by Aimee M. Pavlik

TO THE READER

CAUTION: The writings contained in this handbook
are meant as a source of information, and are not
intended to provide individual medical advice. Such
advice must be obtained from a qualified practitioner.
For all aspects of the treatment program, it is
important that you are heeding the advice of your
doctor, as there are cautions and precautions for each
step.

International Standard Book Number (ISBN): 0-9620479-2-9

A Note From
The Institute for Health Realities

The Institute for Health Realities specializes in tailoring programs according to an individual's own needs and circumstances. Every person has been exposed to different factors throughout their lifetime that can affect their health from environmental, professional, accidental, and even dietary. Our goal is to do away with the "one size fits all" type of health care that many people are given and encourage individual's to take part in gaining and maintaining their own health. We realize the tailored program approach may be out of your capability at this time, however if you follow what is outlined in this book, you will still provide yourself some basic protection.

We want to emphasize that this book is conceptual in nature. The basic concepts and recommendations outlined will benefit any individual who chooses to incorporate them into his/her lifestyle. However, although this basic guide will give you a place to start, we like to encourage every individual to consider a uniquely tailored program designed specifically from his/her own biochemical design.

We hope that after reading this book you will feel equipped with the tools you need to take action and become directly involved in the care you receive. Whether you choose only to try the recommendations outlined in this book or choose to have an individualized profile done, you have stepped onto the road to better health. So, as you read this book, we want to congratulate and encourage you because even if it seems like it is one small step at a time, you are no doubt walking forward into a healthier and happier future.

FOREWORD

With the considerable press coverage regarding toxins in our environment, this book presents vital information that will educate and inform people about mercury (one of the earth's most toxic elements) in a concise and easy-to-read text.

If you are concerned with any of the following questions, this book is a "must read."

Why should mercury be a concern for me?

How can mercury affect me?

Where might mercury be found in my environment?

Should silver-amalgam fillings concern me?

If I decide to have my fillings replaced, how should they be removed and what material should be used to replace them?

What are the symptoms and diseases related to mercury?

What tests can be done to determine if I have been exposed to mercury?

What can I do on a simplified, inexpensive, and generic level to protect myself from mercury's toxic effects?

Sam Queen's ability to present this material in an easy-to-read manner demonstrates why all of us should be concerned with mercury. Encouraging us to make our own decisions, his recommendations help each individual to become educated and therefore proactive in the future of their health.

Paul J. Pavlik, DMD

TABLE OF CONTENTS

THE IV-C MERCURY TOX PROGRAM®

IS THIS BOOK FOR YOU?

Yes, if

> You are concerned that the mercury in your silver-amalgam dental fillings you have, or have had, may be poisoning you.

> You currently have health problems that you and/or your doctor suspect may be due to mercury.

> You've recently undergone standard therapy for acute mercury poisoning possibly from a variety of sources regardless of whether or not your symptoms are still apparent.

If any of these criteria apply to you, you will want to read and implement the treatment program outlined in this book with the help of your doctor.

We want to caution you that the success of your treatment depends on your implementing each step of the program in the correct sequence.

You will need to follow the information enclosed in the proper order and give each step the required amount of time.

Helpful Background Information
Over our lifetime, we are exposed to mercury. It's in the foods we eat, the air we breathe, the water we drink, and the places we work. It is even in the medicine we take and the items we use for decorating our bodies (tattoos, hair dyes, and mascara). Our

exposure to mercury is literally guaranteed, beginning before birth through the placenta and later from our mother's milk.

Due to the many sources of exposure we may encounter, many of us are affected to the point at which we experience symptoms. This is due partly to our lifestyle (food choices, the amount of exercise we engage in, etc.), and partly to our body's genetic, predetermined ability or inability to detoxify mercury.

For these reasons, the amount of mercury each of us can handle before symptoms appear varies from person to person. Your doctor may refer to this as your *mercury threshold*.

If your mercury threshold is high, you could live a lifetime without ever experiencing the symptoms we commonly relate to mercury. Nevertheless, it is possible you may still suffer its effects indirectly due to the fact that high levels of mercury accumulating in the body may worsen the symptoms of any disease or health condition you may come in contact with.

If your mercury threshold is low, it may explain why you react to the slightest mercury exposure.

If you find that you have a low mercury threshold, you need to be especially careful to protect yourself against further exposure by avoiding products, professions, and lifestyle practices that bring you into further contact with mercury.

For this reason, the treatment program outlined in this book will likely benefit everyone who follows it in its entirety.

FREQUENTLY ASKED QUESTIONS

Question: How do I know if mercury is my problem? Are there any tests we can do?

Answer: There <u>are</u> tests for this condition that you and your doctor may decide to conduct. The chapter, *Making a Diagnosis*, addresses this in more detail. Most health care professionals can conduct a risk analysis that matches your symptoms with your history of exposure to mercury. By linking the findings to supporting evidence, your doctor can determine if you are at high risk or low risk.

Question: If mercury is my problem, how do I know if my "silver" amalgam dental fillings are the source of my mercury exposure, or to what extent they contribute to my total risk of mercury exposure?

Answer: Animal studies have demonstrated that dental amalgam fillings are a source of mercury exposure throughout the lifetime of your fillings. The rate of mercury's escape from your filling depends upon its age (newer ones and newly polished ones lose mercury at a faster rate than older ones) and how often you chew or drink hot liquids. Through a mercury vapor analysis, your doctor can determine the rate and amount of mercury coming from your fillings daily. This test is also available through the Institute for Health Realities.

Question: If mercury is shown to be leaking from my fillings in a significant amount, what can I do about it? How do I go about having my amalgams replaced?

Answer: Providing an answer to these questions is the purpose of this book. In addition to following the diet, lifestyle, and food supplement parts of the program, you should probably consider having your amalgams replaced with a less harmful, biocompatible material, in which case you should first ask your dentist to fully explain the various alternatives.

Question: Can I have all of my "silver" amalgam fillings removed at once? And is it necessary to have them replaced in any particular order?

Answer: You can have them replaced all at once if you only have two or three fillings that are small and uncomplicated. If, however, you have a large number of fillings, or if some of them are large and complicated, most mercury-free dentists prefer to work in sections or *quadrants* with appointments spaced about 8-10 days apart. If you have serious health problems, your dentist may want to do a single tooth first to see how you react and to allow a little additional time for the diet, lifestyle, and food supplement program to take effect.

Question: Will my health problems be solved when I replace my fillings? Will I feel better afterwards?

Answer: There is no way at present to tell whether the mercury from your fillings is a cause of any health problems you now have, or may have, in the future. The benefit from replacing these fillings is based solely on the evidence obtained in your risk analysis. Although currently there is no direct relation between mercury and a specific disease, amalgam removal has shown clinical improvements. Some people report experiencing an immediate health improvement while others have reported no appreciable health benefit from having their amalgams replaced. If you are one of those who do not experience immediate improvement, you at least have the satisfaction of knowing that you've removed a known toxin.

Question: I have MS (or arthritis, lupus, or hypothyroidism). Will replacing my amalgam fillings help me, or is such an effort a cruel hoax, as the ADA claims?

Answer: Some people with MS (multiple sclerosis) have had their amalgams replaced as part of their treatment program. Neurologists are in general agreement that MS is an autoimmune disorder, which animal studies show may be caused by mercury or any one of a variety of agents, chemicals and viruses included. If mercury is the cause of your autoimmune disorder, which led you to develop MS, then hypothetically you might expect the progress of your condition to slow or even recede by removing yourself from further exposure. For this reason, many people with MS have chosen to have their amalgam fillings replaced with a non-mercurial alternative. As you might expect, only a few have experienced a dramatic recovery. For those significant few who do, their doctors credit their recovery to spontaneous, "psychological" remission. Yet even those who don't experience dramatic recovery nearly always report feeling better after having gone through the treatment program.

In its various stages, the symptoms of MS and chronic mercury toxicity are strikingly similar. Neither the ADA nor the MS Society has performed any research to assure us that the mercury from dental amalgam hypothesis is true. Yet, because a number of people with MS claim to have experienced some degree of recovery following amalgam replacement, we are encouraging the ADA and the MS Society to study a large number of patients who follow this program. This would compare the course of their disease with MS patients who choose to keep their amalgams.

Refusing to look at this possibility is far crueler to MS patients than denying them the option to see for themselves.

Question: Some people report getting worse after having their amalgams replaced. What's the chance of this happening to me?

Answer: Some people have reported getting worse following amalgam replacement. People who do so are generally those who did not follow a detoxification program beforehand, such as the one discussed in this book, or who did not receive Intravenous Vitamin-C (IV-C) or a chelating agent during or after the appointment. While no one can guarantee this won't happen to you, it stands to reason that if you follow the steps we've outlined, your chances of a good outcome are greatly increased.

Question: Should I simply go out and get my amalgams replaced, or is there something I should know and do beforehand?

Answer: Do not get your amalgams replaced without doing some research first. There are definitely things you should know and do beforehand. Follow the detoxification program outlined in this handbook before, during, and after amalgam removal. Otherwise, the additional mercury spilled during replacement may make your health condition worse. Find an experienced mercury-free dentist to perform your dental work, or find a dentist who is in the process of converting to a mercury-free practice. Such a dentist, in addition to being well versed in the placement and choice of alternative materials, will have equipped his/her office in a manner that protects you, himself/herself, the dental staff, and the environment from additional mercury released during replacement.

Question: What are the best materials to replace my amalgams with? Will these be ADA approved?

Answer: Gold, porcelain, ceramic, and plastic (composite resins) are the accepted materials at the present time. These are ADA-approved. In order to choose the best material for you, it is recommended that you have a biocompatibility test done. This gives you and your dentist a better idea about the material most likely to be compatible with you. (For information on labs that test for biocompatibility, please contact The Institute for Health Realities). Some brief information on each of the types of materials used for crowns ("caps" that cover all or most of the tooth) or bridge attachments are as follows:

- *Metal (gold, etc.):* Metal has an average longevity of 10 years to life, a moderate to high initial cost, and may be used in any location where cosmetics are not a concern. All of the metals are used either as the sole constituent of a crown or as a "thimble" on which porcelain or composite is baked.
- *High noble metal:* Mostly gold with some palladium, silver, and occasionally platinum, zinc, and copper. Gold wears similarly to tooth enamel allowing minimal wear to opposing natural tooth structure.
- *Noble metal:* Mostly palladium with some silver and/or gold. Due to lower noble metal (e.g., gold) content, the cost is less. Since this material is harder than high noble metals, opposing natural tooth structure wears more easily.

- *Base metal*: Mostly nickel with some chrome or cobalt. Although less expensive than high noble or noble metal crowns, it is typically not recommended since it is extremely hard and there exists a high probability of allergic reactions to nickel in the population, especially in women.
- *Porcelain fused to metal*: Average longevity is similar to that of all metal crowns. The porcelain covering can crack when exposed to ice or very hard foods, grinding (bruxing), or clenching. The cost is typically higher since more lab time and materials are required (compared to all metal crowns). Because of porcelain's extreme hardness, it has the tendency to wear down opposing natural tooth structure more rapidly than the all-metal crowns.
- *Ceramic*: Average longevity is similar to that of porcelain to metal crowns, but the ceramic has the same, if not greater, tendency to chip or crack; therefore, ceramic crowns may be used in any area where extreme stress or grinding habits are not a problem. Ceramics are highly esthetic and are indicated in areas where esthetics are important.

The following is a list of materials used for tooth restorations (fillings) when crowns are not necessary:

- *Gold inlays and onlays*: This material has the longest life span with 10 to 15 years or more being normal. They are gold-colored, moderate to high in cost, and may be used in any size restoration in any location where metal does not compromise esthetics. They are very forgiving to opposing teeth since the hardness is similar to natural tooth structure.

- *Composite resin (plastic):* Many variations of this material are on the market today; changes and improvements are occurring constantly. Average longevity is 5 to 10 years. Since they typically have a greater chance to wear down and/or crack, they are best used in medium-to-small sized restorations that are not exposed to severe grinding. Esthetics are excellent since composites are tooth-colored. They may require one or two appointments to place, depending on the material and procedure recommended. These materials are very technique sensitive and require a very different placement protocol when compared to mercury amalgam (silver) fillings; therefore, make sure your dentist has had sufficient training and experience in the use of posterior composite resin fillings.

- *Ceramic/porcelain fillings:* Costs are similar to that of gold, but the esthetic problems found with gold do not exist. They do have a higher tendency to chip or crack if placed in an area of high grinding. Two appointments are typically required for preparation and placement.

- *One-step ceramic (CERAC) fillings or crowns:* These are made from a solid block of ceramic in a computerized milling machine in the dentist's office. Due to the extremely high costs of the equipment and the extra education required, the cost of these fillings/crowns can be equal to or greater than traditional gold, ceramic, or porcelain crowns/fillings. Esthetics may not be quite as good as the traditional porcelains/ceramics since there are a limited number of shades available in the suppliers' inventory. This may change as the demand and popularity of the procedure increases.

Question: Will my dental insurance pay for any of the above materials that my dentist might recommend or that I may desire?

Answer: Dental insurance companies typically have no problem with paying for the replacement of old dental fillings that are chipped, broken, or that have decay underneath the fillings. Unfortunately, to date, most insurance companies do not recognize the need for fillings on posterior teeth to be made of any other material except for amalgam. If this is the case, the insurance will typically approve their usual and customary payment for an amalgam filling replacement or new placement. The patient will then have the choice of what material will be used but will possibly have to pay the difference between the silver filling cost covered by insurance and the cost of the alternative filling material being used. If a crown is needed, and if it is the first time it has been placed on a particular tooth, the insurance company usually will request radiographs (x-rays) and, in certain instances, photographs and models to evaluate the need (from their point of view) for a crown. If the tooth already has a crown or bridge on it, most insurance companies will not pay for a new crown unless the existing crown is at least 5 years old.

Question: I'm already taking vitamins. Can I continue to take these while following the detoxification program described here?

Answer: It's best to stop whatever vitamin program you are now following until afterwards. Following the program in the right order is essential for a good outcome, and some vitamins taken during this process may hinder your success. For instance, Vitamin B complex taken at the beginning of the detoxification program may mask symptoms and/or cause mercury to be converted into a more toxic form. Vitamin B has the ability to methylate mercury, in turn, causing the release and removal of the mercury to be more complicated and possibly more harmful. For this reason, your doctor may also recommend that you withhold from intramuscular (IM) injections of B vitamins until after you've completed the detoxification program.

Other Considerations:

If advanced periodontal disease is present, your dentist will likely suggest that you take steps to correct this problem first. After all, what have you gained from replacing your amalgams if your teeth fall out sometime in the future? Remember, teeth are meant to last a lifetime.

For similar reasons, your dentist may not want to replace a filling in a tooth that has a root canal, or may require a root canal, to save it. The dentist may also find that you have decay and an amalgam build-up under a crown, or a crown made of a non-precious metal that presents a far greater emergency than the simple replacement of an amalgam filling. These things may need to be corrected before your amalgams are replaced.

To truly improve your health, there are many reasons to go slowly; in turn, giving your dentist time to totally assess your dental needs.

• Bear in mind this is a young science, and there's a lot we don't know about biocompatibility. For these reasons, there is no guarantee that the simple replacement of dental amalgam fillings, even with biocompatible materials, will improve your health.

• X-rays are often frowned upon by health-conscious people, and for good reason. Even dentists agree that patients should be protected properly beforehand and that they should not allow themselves to be X-rayed more often than necessary. However, if you refuse this procedure, it may not be possible for your dentist to give you his/her best opinion. It is in your best interest to make sure that your dentist is using the "fastest" x-ray film available, and that the x-ray equipment has been checked and approved by your local state protection agencies. If your dentist is using the newest form of x-ray technology called "digital" radiography, your exposure can be reduced up to 90%.

BACKGROUND ABOUT THIS PROGRAM

What You Need to Know About Amalgam Replacement

People who are clearly mercury-toxic are likely to benefit from amalgam filling replacement and are also likely to benefit from following the detoxification program described in this guide. It is mandatory that you, rather than your doctor, make the decision for amalgam replacement. The exception, of course, is if your doctor has shown you that there is a clear indication that any of your existing amalgam fillings are worn and in need of being replaced. In either case, before your amalgams can be replaced, your doctor may require that you provide him/her with a signed, written consent stating it is your decision to have your amalgams replaced with an alternative material, and that you fully understand the implications of your choice.

Making the best decision for you requires that you read all the material you can on this topic. Once you've made the decision to replace your amalgam fillings, the information found in this book will outline the full detoxification and treatment program that we suggest you follow. These suggestions and concepts have been taken from its companion textbook, **Chronic Mercury Toxicity:** *New Hope Against an Endemic Disease*. This booklet has been written in order to simplify your doctor's instructions and aid you in being educated in the process which you will undergo.

An Overview of Your Treatment Program

If your health is reasonably good but you want your amalgam fillings replaced anyway:

1. Follow the dietary and food supplement portion of the program for a minimum of 2 weeks or more before having your amalgam fillings replaced.
2. Replace your amalgam fillings.
3. Ask your doctor to administer Intravenous Vitamin C (IV-C) during your amalgam replacement or within 24 hours of the procedure.
4. Continue on the dietary and food supplement part of the program for an additional six (6) weeks, or longer if you choose.

If you have a long-standing illness, but are not currently seriously ill, or if you have a variety of food allergies and/ or food sensitivities,

The following step should be added:

5. Your doctor may suggest, or you may request, an additional infusion of IV-C thirty-six (36) or more hours before amalgam replacement.

If you are exceptionally ill from MS or some other disease or condition,

These additional steps may be helpful:

6. Ask your doctor to consider prescribing a heavy metal challenge test using a chelating agent beginning a few days to a week or so after the post amalgam IV-C. It will measure mercury, other heavy metals, and trace minerals in the urine. Ask your doctor to follow the Institute for Health Realities protocol outlined in this book.

7. After the chelating agent has been administered and urine collected, ask your doctor to give you an IV-C infusion.

Post-therapy fatigue

Following treatment with IV-C, and/or a chelating agent, it is not uncommon for someone who was, or is seriously ill to feel fatigued. Getting rid of mercury is only half the battle in getting over its effects. Mercury has the capacity to damage or weaken many cells and to leave the endocrine system in a weakened state. If you suffer from fatigue following your treatment, ask your doctor about various means of boosting your energy level. For additional information on this topic, see the heading "Fatigue" in the chapter titled, *Measuring Your Progress.*

Diet and lifestyle aspects are essential

The importance of following the detoxification program before, during, and after amalgam removal cannot be overemphasized. It accomplishes four important health objectives:

- It assists in breaking mercury loose from cellular binding sites
- It helps to open the channels by which mercury must exit the body
- It assists in repairing damaged cells, tissues, and organ systems, including the endocrine glands and the nervous system
- It helps protect you from any sudden additional exposure to mercury that may result during amalgam replacement, and it aids in the prevention of you becoming worse as a result of amalgam removal.

Intravenous Vitamin C (IV-C) may also be important for complete recovery

An intravenous infusion of vitamin C (IV-C) is highly recommended following (or in some cases during) amalgam removal. Later, it may also be recommended to you following chelation therapy.

A few additional comments about the treatment

There are thousands of people currently suffering from chronic effects of mercury which are a result of a variety of sources for which there has not before been an effective therapy. If you are one of these people, the **IV-C Mercury Tox Program**® is designed to fill this need and offer you hope.

To assist you in making the treatment program as effective as possible, this booklet is meant to educate you and your doctor so that you will both have a better understanding of what the program is meant to do. It will also provide you with a written outline of the detoxification plan that can be referred to as often as necessary.

Before starting this program, please be sure to consult with your doctor as adjustments based on your own case are often necessary. You may also want to suggest two of our books to your doctor as they may find them helpful and informative during this process.

IV-C Mercury Tox Program: A Guide for the Doctor

Standards of Care for Amalgam Removal:
A Guide for the Doctor & Patient

WHAT ARE YOUR SYMPTOMS?

The following are symptoms typically reported by people with chronic mercury toxicity. If you experience any of them, make a note of each one in the space provided on page 29.

Disturbances of the Central Nervous System
- irritability*
- anxiety/nervousness, often with difficulty in breathing
- restlessness
- exaggerated response to stimulation
- fearfulness
- emotional instability*
  - lack of self control
  - fits of anger, with violent, irrational behavior
- loss of self confidence
- indecision
- shyness or timidity, being easily embarrassed
- loss of memory
- inability to concentrate
- lethargy/drowsiness
- insomnia
- mental depression, despondency*
- withdrawal
- suicidal tendencies
- manic-depression
- numbness and tingling of hands, feet, fingers, toes, or lips*
- muscle weakness progressing to paralysis*
- ataxia
- tremors/trembling of hands, feet, lips, eyelids, or tongue*

---

* Classic signs and symptoms of elemental and organic mercury exposure.

25

- poor coordination*
- myoneural transmission failure resembling Myasthenia gravis
- motor neuron disease (ALS/Lou Gehrig's disease)
- multiple sclerosis

Head, Neck, Oral Cavity Disorders
- bleeding gums
- alveolar bone loss
- loosening of teeth
- excessive salivation*
- foul breath*
- metallic taste*
- periodontal disease
- cheilosis
- geographic tongue
- burning sensation, with tingling of lips, face*
- tissue pigmentation (amalgam tattoo of gums)
- leukoplakia
- stomatitis
- ulceration of gingiva, palate, tongue
- dizziness/acute, chronic vertigo
- ringing in the ears
- hearing difficulties
- speech and visual impairment
  - glaucoma
  - restricted, dim vision

Gastrointestinal Effects
- food sensitivities, especially to milk and eggs*
- abdominal cramps, colitis/diverticulitis, or other gastro-intestinal (GI) complaints
- chronic diarrhea/constipation*

---

* Classic signs and symptoms of elemental and organic mercury exposure.

•green or yellow stool

Cardiovascular Effects
•abnormal heart rhythm*
    Characteristic findings on EKG:
    -abnormal changes in the S -T segment
    -lower and broadened P wave
•unexplained, elevated serum triglyceride
•unexplained, elevated cholesterol
•abnormal blood pressure, either high or low

Immunologic & Endocrine
•repeated infections*
    - viral and fungal infections
    - candida or other yeast infections
    - mycobacterial infections
•cancer
•autoimmune disorders*
    - arthritis
    - lupus erythematosis (LE)
    - multiple sclerosis (MS)
•hypothyroidism
•scleroderma
•amyolateral sclerosis (ALS)

Systemic Effects
•chronic headaches
•allergies*
    - severe dermatitis
    - unexplained reactivity
•thyroid disturbance*
•subnormal body temperature*
•cold, clammy skin, especially hands and feet
•excessive perspiration, frequent night sweats*
•unexplained sensory symptoms, including pain
•unexplained numbness, or burning sensations
•unexplained anemia

- G-6-PD deficiency
- adrenal disease
- chronic kidney disease
    - nephrotic syndrome
    - receiving renal dialysis
    - kidney infection
- general fatigue*
- loss of appetite with or without weight loss*
- loss of weight
- hypoglycemia

Children/Infants
- retardation in speech development
- hands and feet red, swollen, and cold
- intelligence disturbances
- slight, persistent fever
- pyramidal symptoms
- mental retardation
- disturbed body growth
- primitive reflexes
- anorexia
- hyperkinesia
- dysarthria
- irritability
- limb deformity
- fretfulness
- weakness
- acrodynia
- autism
- food sensitivities
- cerebral palsy

For a quick referral, make a list here of any symptoms you have that coincide with chronic mercury toxicity. You should attach a copy of this list to your questionnaire.

HAVE YOU BEEN EXPOSED TO MERCURY?

COULD YOU BE AT RISK?

If you are showing adverse health symptoms, and want to know if they may be due to chronic mercury toxicity, the first step in relating your symptoms to mercury is to examine your lifestyle and work habits.

If you are at high risk you will either,

(1) *have a history of exposure through your work,*

(2) *be at risk from certain lifestyle activities, or*

(3) *have or have had at some time in the past, a number of dental amalgam fillings.*

If you regularly come in contact with mercury, and if you have symptoms consistent with chronic mercury toxicity, then you are a likely candidate for this treatment program.

A history of working in or making a hobby of any of the professions listed alphabetically on the following pages, would be an indication that you have been exposed to mercury and may even be at high risk. Read over the list carefully and check those that apply to you. Then, answer the questions at the end.

Professions and/or Hobbies

___ acetic acid makers
___ amalgam makers
___ bacteriocidal makers
___ barometer makers
___ battery makers

31

___ bronzers

___ construction workers who handle dry wall
or spackling materials

___ calibration instrument makers

___ caustic soda makers

___ ceramic workers

___ chlorine makers

___ coal furnace operators, especially those
who operate coal-burning electric utility
furnaces

___ commercial and sport fishermen and their
families who eat 3 or more servings of
fish weekly of the types listed below:

> Large, predator fish
> -salt water: swordfish, halibut, tuna
> -fresh water: bass, northern pike, walleye
> Scavenger fish/bottom feeders
> -salt water: lobster, shrimp, shellfish
> -fresh water: alligator, catfish

___ crematorium operators, or if you live near
one

___ dental amalgam makers

___ dental office personnel

___ dentists

___ direct current meter workers

___ disinfectant makers

___ drug makers

___ drywall installers (nail cover-up cement
and joint compound both contain
mercury)

___ dye makers

___ electric apparatus makers

___ electroplaters

___ embalmers

___ explosive makers

___ farmers

___ fingerprint detectors

___ fireworks makers

___ fishermen

___ fungicide makers

___ fur processors

___ gold extractors

___ histology technicians

___ incinerator operators and people who live near a community incinerator that processes discarded items rich in mercury, such as:
- -batteries
- -latex paint
- -fluorescent lights
- -plastics

___ ink makers

___ insecticide makers

___ instrument calibration technicians

___ jewelers

___ laboratory workers
- - clinical
- - chemical

___ lamp makers
- - fluorescent
- - mercury arc

___ manometer makers

___ mercury workers
- - miners
- - refiners

___ neon light makers

___ paint makers

___ painters
- - whether you are a professional, or have just recently painted your own home, inside or outside

___ paper pulp workers, and those who eat fish caught downstream from a paper pulp mill

___ percussion cap makers and loaders

___ pesticide users
- - farmers
- - gardeners

- landscapers
- manufacturers
- plant shop personnel
___ photographers
___ printers
___ pressure gauge makers
___ seed handlers
___ silver extractors
___ spackling handlers or manufacturers
(dry wall cement, joint compound, nail
cover-up material all contain mercury)
___ tannery workers
___ taxidermists
___ thermometer makers
___ vinyl chloride makers
___ wood preservative workers

Here are some other sources of possible mercury exposure:

___ contact lens solutions containing
thimerosal (merthiolate)
___ vaccines containing thimerosal
___ laxatives containing calomel
___ mascara (the water proof variety)
___ Mercurochrome (especially when applied
to an extensive open wound)
thimerosal (merthiolate)
___ Preparation H
___ skin lightening creams
___ surgical sutures
(suspect mercury if you feel you are "allergic" to
sutures)
___ tattoos with red in the dye
(suspect mercury if you demonstrate a
sensitivity to the dye)
___ vaginal gels

If any of the professions, activities or products listed apply to you, make sure to indicate it below as well as when filling out your health questionnaire.

Have you been exposed to mercury on the job?
Yes_____   No_____   Don't Know_____

If yes,when? _____
_____

What profession were you in?_____
_____
_____

Explain your exposure:_____
_____
_____
_____

List any activities you do or have participated in that might have exposed you to mercury:_____
_____
_____
_____
_____

List any products you use that might have exposed you to mercury:_____
_____
_____
_____

Do you presently have dental amalgam fillings?
Yes_____   No_____   How many?_____

If no, have you ever? Yes_____   No_____

If yes, how long ago?_____   How many? _____

MAKING A DIAGNOSIS

Risk Assessment
Before your doctor can treat you for chronic mercury toxicity, he/she must first connect your symptoms with those commonly attributed to mercury. These symptoms must then be linked to your history of exposure. If a connection is made, then your doctor has sufficient reason to offer you treatment.

Mercury Vapor Analysis
If dental amalgam fillings are part of your exposure, this simple test, although not in itself diagnostic, can tell how much mercury is leaking from your amalgams and to what extent your health is at risk from exposure.

For the test, your doctor will likely instruct you to do the following:

DO NOT DO BEFORE OR DURING THE TEST:

DO NOT eat, drink, chew gum, smoke, brush your teeth, or engage in any other activity that may cause a stimulation or disruption to the surfaces of the amalgams for a full 90 minutes before your appointment. Also, DO NOT eat garlic or take any garlic supplement the day of the test.

THINGS TO REMEMBER DURING THE TEST:

Breathe only through your nose (if there is even a need to breathe during the short time the test is in progress). Swallow hard just before starting. This clears the mouth and pharynx of air and saliva. Then, open wide and hold that position for the duration of the test cycle (10 seconds) while your dentist waves the instrument around inside your mouth. This gives your dentist a control reading, which indicates the baseline, unstimulated release of mercury vapor given off naturally from parts of your body other than dental amalgam fillings.

At this point you will be given a piece of sugarless chewing gum and asked to chew normally for 10 minutes using both sides of your mouth. At the end of 10 minutes, you'll be asked to remove the gum, swallow hard, open wide, and breathe through your nose. Your doctor will again take a reading and probably repeat the procedure more than once.

What the Readings Mean
The first reading will give you and your doctor a sense of the significance of your results by comparing your reading to several exposure limits set by branches of the U.S. government.[1] If your raw reading exceeds 30 mcg/cum. (which tends to be an average reading for most amalgam patients after 10 minutes of chewing) then it is apparent you are being exposed to mercury vapor at a level exceeding air quality standards set by the federal government.

Once your risk of exposure has been assessed, you and your doctor will have a sound basis for whether or not to pursue the matter further.

The Diagnosis
There are several ways people can become mercury toxic. Various forms of mercury toxicity are listed on the following pages.

------

[1] The average patient with 5 fillings receives an average daily dose of 9-10 mcg of mercury, the equivalent of 45-50 mcg per five days, or 63-70 mcg per seven days. This exceeds OSHA'S Threshold Limit Value (TLV) of 50 mcg set for those who work a 40-hour week.

Minamata Disease

Individuals who suffer from such exposure manifest severe tremors and probably experience convulsions and dementia as well as dysfunction of any or all of the body's major systems. The classic example of this is the Minamata Bay incident in which an entire village in Japan was exposed by eating fish contaminated by a manufacturing plant's mercury waste. Minamata Disease has since become the official label assigned to people who are poisoned by methyl mercury. The traditional term, mercury poisoning, is still used for Minamata Disease but is also used to describe the effects of acute poisoning from other mercury sources.

Methyl Mercury, Mercury Vapor and Inorganic Mercury

Some people claim amalgam fillings do not cause disease because the classic signs of mercury poisoning have not been demonstrated. This claim is accurate, but misleading. Amalgam fillings do not cause you to be exposed to methyl mercury, rather, amalgam brings about a chronic exposure to two different forms of mercury—mercury vapor and inorganic mercury.

Inorganic mercury exits the filling and enters the surrounding soft tissues through a process known as oral galvanism. This occurs when the mouth is very acidic. The presence of a purple "tattoo" on the gumline above the filling is evidence of this happening.

Micromercurialism

Poisoning from mercury vapors, termed micromercurialism, was described in 1969 by a Russian scientist, I.M. Trachtenburg. Like Minamata Disease, it does not accurately describe the effect of chronic, low-dose exposure to the two forms of mercury arising from amalgam fillings. Making matters worse, people who are exposed to mercury from dental fillings frequently receive chronic exposure from other sources. Such as methyl mercury from fish as well as a variety of medications such as hemorrhoid preparations. When observed from this point of view, the symptoms of low-dose, chronic exposure to mercury from a variety of mercury sources does not fit any of the patterns of mercury poisoning.

Chronic Mercury Toxicity

To more accurately describe the many overlapping symptoms of chronic mercury exposure, H.L. "Sam" Queen coined the term _chronic mercury toxicity_. This term describes what is observed in most individuals who are exposed to the two sources of mercury from dental fillings, as well as methyl and phenyl mercury. Phenyl mercury is mainly used in research and is in phenolic compounds used to scrub down intensive care units.

Chronic mercury toxicity can manifest in a variety of symptoms but will particularly show up as one or more of the six sub-clinical defects common to all chronic disease. Through the manifestation of these sub-clinical conditions, exposure to mercury from dental fillings may heighten susceptibility to infections and contribute to a host of degenerative diseases, including, autoimmune disorders.

At this point in history, there is only one definitive test that can determine your symptoms (past, present, or future) are due to mercury. It is the _Porphyrin Profile Test_. However, there are a number of other tests doctors can use to support their diagnosis. The following is a description of those tests.

<u>The Porphyrin Profile Test</u>, is being performed by James Woods, Ph.D., at the University of Washington in Seattle, WA. Porphyrins are formed in body tissues as part of normal metabolic processes. Porphyrins not used for metabolism are excreted in the urine in a well-defined pattern. Mercury alters this pattern in a way that is directly proportional to the amount of mercury accumulated in the body. Therefore, the Porphyrin Profile test is a bioindicator of mercury body burden. This test is best used to detect mercury in the body as a result of long-term occupational use or from environmental exposure (i.e., hazardous waste sites).

<u>Blood and unchallenged urine mercury levels</u>
Although often recommended, these are of limited value in diagnosing chronic mercury toxicity. An elevated blood and urine level is seldom seen probably because blood mercury is either excreted or channeled to tissues without signaling a substantial rise or fall in the blood level. For reasons largely unknown, the kidneys fail to excrete mercury as they would normally in response to a substantial, acute mercury exposure.

<u>Hair analysis</u> is also popularly used. Although more reliable than blood and urine mercury levels, it is still not adequate for making a diagnosis. It can, however, be used to confirm one. Hair analysis is better at measuring methyl mercury levels (as from fish) as opposed to mercury vapor (from amalgam fillings).

<u>The ELISA ACT Test for Hypersensitivity</u> is intended to help identify those people who are hypersensitive to mercury. Since hypersensitivity is a marker of autoimmune disease, this test may ultimately be important to people with MS and other autoimmune related disorders who want to know if mercury has

caused or contributed to their disease. It also may be beneficial to those who are at high risk for developing these diseases.

Mercury Challenge Test: If further testing is desired, you and your doctor might consider doing a "challenge" test. This consists of giving a chelating agent, such as DMSA, DMPS, EDTA or D-Penicillamine (Cuprin™ or D-Pen™) to see if mercury in the urine increases in response to the challenge. A positive challenge test confirmed by your symptoms and history of exposure offers sufficient supportive evidence for diagnosis. Here at the Institute for Health Realities we do not recommend having a challenge test while you have amalgam fillings because of the chance of mercury leaching from the fillings, especially if your mouth is acidic. However, through nutritional preparation, you may be able to prepare your body for the test. If you elect to have this test, your doctor will ask you to first empty your bladder. Then, he/she will administer the chelating agent. Make sure you drink large amounts of water prior to and during the administering of the chelating agent. After the chelating agent has been administered, you will collect your urine and submit it to a clinical laboratory for analysis of heavy metals.

Interpretation: A rise in the urine assay for heavy metals will be seen in nearly everyone even without symptoms. However, if you have a significant amount of mercury stored in your tissue, and symptoms to match, the second urine collection should demonstrate a 2-fold to 10-fold rise in the content of particular heavy metals, especially mercury. A repeat challenge test can be given later to evaluate therapy.
NOTE: D-Penicillamine is a drug that has long been used as an effective therapy treatment of acute heavy

metal poisoning. However, we <u>do not</u> recommend its use in this treatment program other than what may be necessary to perform the challenge test. Any long-term use of this drug may result in unwanted side effects that often occur.

<u>Blood Tests:</u> Beyond the challenge test method, there are few accepted methods for determining chronic mercury toxicity. However, people who utilize one of many Institute for Health Realities (IHR) strategies, along with this program, will achieve optimum results. Our extensive blood and urine tests allow our consultants to see toxic "footprints", whether from mercury, another heavy metal, an organic solvent, a petrochemical, radiation, or a pesticide. A sampling of these tests include: IgM, Immunoglobulins, lipid profile, protein, BUN, Cortisol, and the Beta-2 Microglobulin, Serum and Urine. This last test is OSHA's standard test to determine if someone should be removed from the workplace due to metal poisoning.

In addition, the IHR chemistry panels will include testing required to determine your candidacy for the IV-C program, or at least how to guide you so that you may become a candidate.

Once your diagnosis is made, you are ready to go on to the dietary and lifestyle aspect of the treatment program.

THE DETOX PROGRAM

The dietary aspect of the **IV-C Mercury Tox Program**® places an emphasis on eggs and cultured dairy foods because of their benefit to people whose nerves, emotions, and brain cells have been impaired.

Typically, people who are mercury toxic, develop sensitivities to milk and eggs that doctors often refer to as lactose intolerance. Many people affected complain of chronic yeast problems as well. These, and many other symptoms ranging from allergies, infections, and a myriad of disease conditions, often begin through mercury's initial disruption of the bacteria normally residing in the gastrointestinal tract. For this reason, re-establishing this balance is necessary for recovering from any condition caused by chronic mercury toxicity.

Even people who have no apparent problems with their gastrointestinal tract or yeast, seem to make better progress if they utilize the part of the program intended to balance the digestive system. Because of this fact, every person begins at the same point.

During this Detox Program, be sure to note the foods you are to avoid in the chapter, *Food Recommendations*, as this is important to the effectiveness of the program.

The following dosages are based on a 150 lb. person.

THE DETOX PROGRAM

NOTE: *You must be at the Day 10 point in the Program at least 1 week prior to your scheduled amalgam removal.*

Days 1, 2, & 3

Morning:
- 2 T. of fresh lemon juice in water
- 500 mg essential garlic oil
- 1 capsule *lactobacillus* supplement[2]

30 min. after dinner:
- 2 T. of fresh lemon juice in water
- 500 mg essential garlic oil
- 1 capsule *lactobacillus* supplement

Bedtime:
- 2 T. of fresh lemon juice in water
- 500 mg essential garlic oil
- 1 capsule *lactobacillus* supplement

Day 4, 5 & 6

Morning:
- 2 T. of fresh lemon juice in water
- 500 mg essential garlic oil
- 1 capsule *lactobacillus* supplement
- Break open 1 capsule lactobacillus supplement and sprinkle contents into 1/2 cup cottage cheese or plain organic yogurt.

---

[2] It's important to get a high quality, refrigerated friendly bacteria. If you have yeast infections we recommend "Pro-Biotic" by Klaire Laboratories. It is available through the Institute for Health Realities.

30 min. after dinner:
- 2 T. of fresh lemon juice in water
- 500 mg essential garlic oil
- 1 capsule *lactobacillus* supplement

Bedtime:
- 2 T. of fresh lemon juice in water
- 500 mg essential garlic oil
- 1 capsule *lactobacillus* supplement

If gastric distress occurs, start over with Days 1 - 3.

Day 7, 8 & 9

Morning:
- 2 T. of fresh lemon juice in water
- 500 mg essential garlic oil
- 1 capsule *lactobacillus* supplement
- Break open 1 capsule lactobacillus supplement and sprinkle contents into 1/2 cup cottage cheese or plain organic yogurt.

Afternoon:
- Break open 1 capsule lactobacillus supplement and sprinkle contents into 1/2 cup of cottage cheese or plain organic yogurt.

30 min. after dinner:
- 2 T. of fresh lemon juice in water
- 500 mg essential garlic oil
- 1 capsule *lactobacillus* supplement

Bedtime:
- 2 T. of fresh lemon juice in water
- 500 mg essential garlic oil
- 1 capsule *lactobacillus* supplement

If gastric distress occurs, start over with Days 4 - 6

Day 10

This part of the detoxification program must be started at least 1 week prior to amalgam removal.

At this point, any problems you may have had with yeast should have cleared up and if so, you may introduce red meat back into your diet. If your yeast problem is still present, continue to avoid red meats.

If you are lactose intolerant and have successfully made it to Day 10 without gastric distress, you may continue on. If you are still having gastric distress, start over with Days 1 - 3 until your gastric distress subsides. Little to no gastric distress is a sign that your gastrointestinal tract has regained enough of a balance to handle the rest of the Program.

Upon reaching Day 10, your program will consist of the following for the duration of the time prior to your amalgam removal:

Morning:
- 2 T. of fresh lemon juice in water
- 500 mg essential garlic oil
- 1 capsule *lactobacillus* supplement[3]
- Break open 1 capsule lactobacillus supplement and sprinkle contents into 1/2 cup cottage cheese or plain organic yogurt.

Afternoon:
- Break open 1 capsule lactobacillus supplement and sprinkle contents into 1/2 cup of cottage cheese or plain organic yogurt.

---

[3] It's important to get a high quality, refrigerated friendly bacteria. If you have yeast infections we recommend "Pro-Biotic" by Klaire Laboratories. It is available through the Institute for Health Realities.

30 min. after dinner:
- 2 T. of fresh lemon juice in water
- 500 mg essential garlic oil
- 1 capsule *lactobacillus* supplement

Bedtime:
- 2 T. of fresh lemon juice in water
- 500 mg essential garlic oil
- 1 capsule *lactobacillus* supplement

FOOD RECOMMENDATIONS

The following is a list of food to include and/or avoid in your diet during the Detox Program. Note that when looking at the different items listed, these are suggestions for items to eat throughout the day. In other words, you may choose 3 items under the "Cultured Dairy Products" category and have 1 serving of each. For poultry products such as chicken or lamb, a serving size can be measured to be the equivalent size of a deck of cards.

A note on EGGS:
Eggs are extremely important to anyone whose nerves and/or brain has been affected by mercury. If you are so affected (the lone exception being stroke patients), eggs should become your major source of protein. Reintroducing eggs to your diet when you are highly sensitive or lactose intolerant can be difficult. (Refer to the Detox Program chapter for detailed instructions) You may also want to begin reintroducing yourself with raw eggs blended in juice and yogurt. You may even want to add some vanilla for flavor. Raw eggs have the advantage of providing free amino acids, which are much more easily digested than complex proteins.[4] Steaming, boiling, poaching, or scrambling eggs is also recommended. Never overcook eggs or fry them in animal fat or margarine.

---

[4] Because one-third of 56 major outbreaks of salmonella food poisoning last year was linked to contaminated, uncooked eggs, the FDA has designated eggs a "potentially hazardous food." Under this designation, we are obligated to recommend cooked eggs. However, in people who have reestablished the normal balance of gastrointestinal bacteria, the risk of salmonella infection is greatly reduced. By following this program as outlined, the potential benefit of raw eggs far outweighs the risk.

CAUTION: It is **very important** that anyone who is consuming large quantities of eggs also be supplementing with vitamin C, eating lots of fiber, exercising regularly, is not constipated, and does not have a history of stroke.

One final note: The concern is often raised that chickens are fed fishmeal and that chicken and eggs may become a potential source of mercury toxicity. By definition, fishmeal is made of anchovies, which are harvested off the west coast of Peru. This area usually does not have a problem with mercury contamination. In addition, anchovies are smaller fish at the lower end of the food chain; therefore, containing the least amount of mercury.

INCLUDE these Foods	Servings
Cultured Dairy Products	3 servings daily
yogurt	
cottage cheese	
buttermilk	
kefir	
soft cheeses	
- Havarti - Bleu	
- Brie - Monterey Jack	
- Mozzarella - Swiss	
- Munster - Jarlsberg	
Fresh Lemon Juice	2 T. in the morning 2 T. at night
Whole Garlic	as often as possible add to cooking
Onion (raw or cooked)	as often as possible

52

Whole Grain Products[5]
    breads
    flours
    pastas

1 serving daily

Manganese-Rich Foods
    oatmeal
    brown rice
    peas
    beans

1 serving daily
(app. 1/2 cup)

Fresh Fruits & Vegetables

4-8 servings daily
(app. 1/2 cup)

Protein
    poultry (skinless)
    lamb
    eggs

2 servings daily

Unprocessed Vegetable Oils
    salads
    cooking

No more than 2 T.
per day

**Papaya, Pineapple, Kiwi,
Mango, or Sprouts**
(an occasional serving of beets)

1 serving daily

Sunflower Seeds
    raw, unsalted

1 T. per day

Butter

No more than
1/4 lb. a day

---

[5] If you have arthritis, undiagnosed joint pain, or sensitivities to whole oats or wheat, it is advisable to limit your whole grain choices to short-grain brown rice.

AVOID these Foods
NO red meat
NO foods containing refined sugar[6]
NO milk (use acidophilus milk if it is necessary)
NO deep-fried foods
NO seafood or fresh water fish
      * except Alaskan salmon
NO white flour products (bread, flour or pasta)
NO margarine
LIMIT caffeine and alcohol intake

Food Supplements[7]	Amount

Lactobacillus acidophilus
   1 per serving of
   cultured dairy foods
   or on an empty stomach
	3 capsules daily

Essential oil of garlic
   (not garlic powder)
   on empty stomach
	3 capsules daily

Zinc
  * sunflower seeds are a
    a natural source of zinc
  * zinc helps promote
    healing and fight infections
	30 mg daily

---

[6]Refined sugar is often a hidden ingredient. Most yogurts, cereals, and other packaged foods contain sugar. It is wise to shop at health food stores during the Detox program, although healthy alternatives such as Mountain High® yogurt and **Nutri-Grain**® cereals are available in many supermarkets. Replace refined sugar with raw honey, pure maple syrup, or date sugar.

[7] The various supplements mentioned here can be purchased through the Institute for Health Realities (719) 598-4968.

Glutothione:	300 mg daily
* Only for people who are not allergic to more than 2 foods.	
Vitamin E	400 I.U. daily
Black Current Seed Oil	2 caps daily
Salmon Oil	2 caps daily

2 Weeks Following Amalgam Removal

Continue with the diet and supplement program. If you are seriously ill, you may need to remain on the program for anywhere from 6 weeks to 6 months depending on your progress. A longer period will be required if your symptoms persist. In either case, consult with your doctor to adjust diet and supplements to your needs.

Hopefully, at the end of the detoxification period, not only will you be free of adverse symptoms, but your health will be much improved and you will be on your way to enjoying a healthier lifestyle.

LIFESTYLE RECOMMENDATIONS

A successful Detox program will enable your body to rid itself of mercury in the most safe and efficient way. We want to reiterate the importance of listening to the advice of your doctor during this process as there are aspects of this and other treatment programs that require the educated and informed decision of both doctor and patient. The following are other suggestions for your consideration; however, again, the advice of a health care professional should be sought out prior to participating in any of the below.

Bowel cleanse: If you are constipated, you may want to consider a bowel cleanse. Bowel cleanse packets are available at most health food stores.

Titrate to bowel tolerance with vitamin C: This may be used afterwards, or instead of a bowel cleanse. Again, check first with your doctor as he/she will need to determine if it is safe for you. A history of kidney dysfunction, kidney stones, diabetes, or G-6-PD deficiency may exclude you from this option. The object is to saturate the tissues with vitamin C as quickly as possible.

Begin by taking 2 grams of vitamin C with water first thing in the morning (add a squeeze of lemon juice to the water). The vitamin C source should be ascorbic acid, but sodium ascorbate can be used if you have an ulcer, esophagitis, colitis, or related intestinal problems.

Every 15 minutes for the remainder of the day, take an additional 2 grams of vitamin C with lemon water. Continue until you experience diarrhea. A normal bowel movement, or gas, is not the endpoint. Make sure you experience diarrhea before stopping. When symptoms first appear, discontinue taking the vitamin C and record the total amount you've taken. If you don't get results by bedtime, start the process over the following day using 3 grams every 15 minutes. To stop the diarrhea, take 2 caps of activated charcoal (approximately 250mg charcoal per capsule). If needed, you can take 1 cap every hour until the diarrhea stops.

Interpreting the results: 80% of adults will tolerate 10 to 15 grams of vitamin C without having diarrhea. Those who are seriously ill with chronic mercury toxicity will tolerate a much larger dosage, ranging up to 50 or 100 grams daily. Diarrhea will occur when your body has all the vitamin C it needs. When the intestines will not absorb any more vitamin C, the vitamin C travels further into the lower colon or rectum where it creates a hypertonic situation; thereby, producing diarrhea in much the same way as a water enema.

NOTE: Intravenous vitamin C (IV-C) does not cause diarrhea because it doesn't enter the colon. It does, however, reduce the amount of oral vitamin C required to cause gastric symptoms. For this reason you are advised to withhold taking oral vitamin C until an hour or so after the IV-C infusion is completed.

As your health improves, the amount of vitamin C required to induce gastric symptoms markedly subsides. This is why "titrating to bowel tolerance" is an excellent parameter for evaluating your improvement.

Kidney cleanse: Drink 6 or more glasses of water daily, enough so that you have to urinate 6 or more times throughout the day.

Promote perspiration: Use a sauna 3 to 5 times weekly. Remain in the sauna until perspiration begins all over your body. Step out and take a cool shower, then return to the sauna. Repeat the sauna/shower cycle three times per visit. <u>Pregnant women and patients with cardiovascular disease should not engage in this exercise without their doctor's advice</u>. Always consume electrolyte replacement foods beforehand such as grape or prune juice as well as cultured dairy foods. Also, make sure to drink plenty of water.

Night sweats: If you experience night sweats, get up and take a cool shower after each episode. Change your bed linens before returning to bed.

Physical activity: Engage in some form of daily exercise according to your physical ability. If you are physically able, 20-30 minutes of aerobic activity (jogging, walking, bicycling, or swimming) per day is ideal. Shower immediately afterwards.

Detox Bath: Take a detox bath by soaking 20 minutes in 104-105°F water with the following:

Days 1 and 2: 1 cup baking soda only
Days 3 and 4: 1/2 cup baking soda
                    1/2 cup Epsom salts
Days 5 and 6: 1 cup Epsom salts only

Repeat no more often than 2 times per month; otherwise, you will need to supplement with a broad spectrum trace mineral.

If you have skin problems:
Add 1-tablespoon comfrey root powder to each bath.

Epsom salts, also known as bitter salts, or heptahydrate, is mostly magnesium sulfate. It occurs in nature as epsomite, and has a very high-density (1.67). At 80°F it will lose 4H2O. At 100°F it will lose 5H2O. This latter property is why it is used in the detox bath. As water is lost from magnesium in a hot bath, the resulting higher concentration causes water to be pulled out through the body pores. Toxins then come out with the water.

Other: Make yourself aware of the many potential sources of mercury in your immediate environment other than dental amalgam fillings. Learn to ask questions before making purchases, or avoid products that historically contain mercury.

AMALGAM REPLACEMENT

Choosing the replacement material
If you believe you are highly reactive to your present fillings or to various metals, plastics, or chemicals, it is wise to do a compatibility study before replacing your amalgams with an alternative material. Your doctor can advise you on the method and cost for doing this.

If your funds are limited, or if you have no history of sensitivity to metals or chemicals commonly used in dentistry, then you might consider bypassing the biocompatibility studies. This is a decision that you and your dentist can make during your initial evaluation.

On the day your amalgams are to be replaced

DO NOT take oral vitamin C supplements the morning of your appointment. Wait until after the anesthetic procedure is completed. Vitamin C may prevent the local anesthetic from taking effect, or hinder the length of its effectiveness.

For similar reasons do not ask your doctor to give you an intravenous infusion of vitamin C (IV-C) for 36 hours before the dental procedure, as it too may interfere with your anesthesia.

If IV-C is given *during* the dental procedure, as we recommend, your doctor knows to start the infusion after he/she has anesthetized your mouth. He/she may otherwise suggest that you wait until afterwards to receive your IV-C, which is quite acceptable.

Characteristically, your mercury-free dentist will use safeguards during amalgam removal. Some of the ones you might see are:

- Large amounts of water and high volume suction
- Good ventilation
- A protective nosepiece that draws air from another room, from outside, or from a nitrous oxide /oxygen tank
- A protective drape
- Protective glasses
- A Rubber dam
- He/She will cut each amalgam in sections first and lift out the chunks rather than simply grinding out the entire filling. This serves to minimize the mercury "mist" that inevitably occurs during replacement.
- If you or your dentist are concerned about possible ingestion of amalgam particles or dust during the amalgam removal, it is recommended that you take an activated charcoal capsule immediately prior to the procedure.

RECEIVING IV-C

Intravenous vitamin C (IV-C) is fast becoming a standard in the treatment of patients with chronic mercury toxicity. There are many possible reasons for IV-C's effectiveness one of which is that ultra large doses serve to scavenge for disease and free radicals that would otherwise destroy normal protective mechanisms. Since mercury carries out its destructive role through production of free radicals, the function of ascorbate in protecting you from these agents is reason enough to justify the use of IV-C in your treatment.

Additional functions of IV-C include:

- It supports dietary measures in breaking mercury loose from its bonding sites within the body
- It protects the body from the potential damage that mercury might cause while being excreted
- It reduces mercury's affinity for binding to other cells while it is being excreted
- It promotes the healing process

CAUTION: As with any therapeutic treatment or intervention, there are always possible side effects and risks that need to be considered. If you currently have, or have ever had, any of the conditions listed below, you may not be a candidate for IV-C during your treatment due to possible complications. Whether you have been able to control your condition or not will also play a role in determining your candidacy. Having a blood chemistry performed may be helpful in determining your candidacy.

Diabetes (insulin-dependent)
Kidney disease
Pregnancy

Reduced kidney function
Kidney stones
History of kidney stones
Urinary tract infection
History of chronic anemia due to G-6-PD deficiency

If you are found to be a candidate for this part of the treatment program, your doctor will infuse IV-C using the following calculation:

750 mg / kg body weight = dosage

<u>Example</u>
If you are 110 lbs., you will receive 37.5 g IV-C.

110 lbs. ÷ 2.2 = 50 kg
50 kg x 750 mg (0.75 g) = <u>37.5 g IV-C</u>

Physicians who are unfamiliar with the rationale behind the **IV-C Mercury Tox Program**® may unknowingly compromise the benefit of IV-C by substituting a few grams of IV-C with EDTA, calcium, magnesium, vitamin B_{12}, and/or other IV nutrients. While this practice is beneficial to you in many ways, evidence raises doubts over EDTA's ability to rid the body of mercury.[8]

The doctor should use Lactated Ringer's solution as the parenteral fluid for the IV-C. This is the safest parenteral fluid available. There are some risks to using other parenteral fluids such as D5W (Dextrose 5% in water).

---

[8] Riordan, H., and Cheraskin, E., "Mineral Excretion Associated with EDTA Chelation Therapy," *Journal Adv. Med.*, 3(2): 111-123, 1990.

What <u>you should know.</u>

- You should know what the high-risk conditions are.
- You should know that you must make every effort possible to deal with medium risk conditions beforehand, such as correcting a urinary tract infection.
- You should follow the protective diet and lifestyle program.
- You will hopefully continue following this regimen for at least a week following your IV-C.

You are also advised to:

- Dress comfortably, but warmly, on the day you receive your infusion, as IV-C can cause a slight chill.
- Drink plenty of water before the IV-C so you will be well hydrated
- Bring someone with you to drive home, as IV-C can sometimes leave you feeling a little light-headed afterwards (this may last up to 30 minutes)
- Drink 2 T. of fresh lemon juice in water or fruit juice early in the day when you receive your IV-C. Bring some additional natural fruit juice with you to drink during the IV-C should you feel shaky.
- Inform the IV nurse immediately if you develop a slight headache, dizziness, or feel shaky. These symptoms will let the nurse know that the rate of infusion needs to be adjusted.
- Ask for water during the IV-C whenever you feel thirsty.
- Continue taking oral vitamin C supplements for a prescribed period of time following the IV-C to

prevent rebound scurvy-like symptoms.[9]

Does the Program Require Multiple Infusions?
Most people who have their amalgams replaced will require only one IV-C infusion per quadrant of amalgams removed. People who are seriously ill may require additional infusions.

---

[9] NOTE: IV-C does not cause diarrhea because it does not enter the colon. It does, however, reduce the amount of oral vitamin C required to cause gastric symptoms. For this reason you are advised to not resume taking your oral vitamin C until an hour or so after the infusion is completed.

MEASURING YOUR PROGRESS

A number of tests may be used to evaluate your improvement after completion of the **IV-C Mercury Tox Program.**® The first and most commonly used is subjective reporting, in other words, how you feel.

A more scientific approach may be to look at before and after test results by ordering blood, urine, psychological, and neurological evaluations prior to and following the treatment program.

While there are many other means of evaluating your improvement, each of which would be based upon your initial health symptoms, the following would apply to nearly every mercury toxic patient.

Your improvement may be indicated by:

A reduction in any of the following:
- Challenge Test for mercury
- drop in IgM
- normalizing of BUN and Beta 2 Microglobulin
- Blood cortisol levels (a decrease in the fasting blood cortisol following treatment indicates a general reduction in stress
- bowel tolerance to megadose oral vitamin C

An increase in:
- appetite
- body weight

Positive changes in:
- Porphyrin Profile test (currently under development)
- hypersensitivity testing (i.e.ELISA ACT)

Positive changes in:
- lipid profile
- electrocardiogram (EKG)
- electroencephalogram (EEG)
- brain scan
- personality and psychological inventory test
- white blood cell count
- white blood cell differential
  T-lymphocyte count
  B-lymphocyte count

If you experience Fatigue:
It is not uncommon for fatigue to persist long after mercury has exited your body. This is partially due to the effect mercury has on organs and organ systems. If this is your situation, you may want to consider one of IHR's comprehensive blood chemistries. If you decide to handle it independently, you may want to try the following:

- Neutra-Phos   1 packet daily

- Alka- Seltzer Gold©   1 packet daily

- Co-Enzyme Q-10   50-100 mg daily
  Especially effective if mercury has left your heart muscle weak

- Adrenal extract   2 drops daily
  Administered under the tongue

- Daily oral vitamin B   25-50 mg each

- Broad spectrum   1 daily
  mineral supplement:
  Low in vitamin D and calcium without iron

- Raw thyroid extract   1/2 grain daily

- Electrical depolarizer
Carry in shirt pocket to counter electrical smog that may be absorbing or utilizing necessary cell energy

The following need to be prescribed by your doctor:

- Protamine   3 units/day
For the zinc insulin (PZI) non-diabetic, especially effective in normalizing low blood pressure

- B vitamins[10]   Intramuscular (IM)
Injections, twice weekly, or as needed, consisting of:

Vitamin B_{12}	1 cc (as hydroxocobalamin)
B Complex	1 cc
Folic Acid	0.5 cc

---

[10] Many injectables are preserved with a mercury-based preservative (thimerosal). Your mercury-free doctor should be aware of this problem and obtain only mercury-free injectables.

CONGRATULATIONS!

Now that you've completed the **IV-C Mercury Tox Program**,® we'd like to hear from you. Tell us briefly how you became exposed to mercury, what your symptoms were before you began the program, and how they compare with your health today. In addition, we'd like to hear any comments you might have that would make the program easier to follow. By sharing your experiences with us, you will have contributed to the ever-growing body of knowledge that's accumulating on this topic.

Send your comments to:

Institute for Health Realities
Attn: IV-C Mercury Tox Program
5245 Centennial Blvd., Suite 100
Colorado Springs, CO, 80919
USA

FURTHER INFORMATION

PRODUCTS AND SERVICES
THE INSTITUTE FOR HEALTH REALITIES

The IV-C Mercury Tox Program: A Guide for the Doctor
This is a companion booklet to the medical reference text *Chronic Mercury Toxicity: New Hope Against an Endemic Disease*. The text, by H.L."Sam" Queen, is a 300-page, well-referenced and indexed guide for the doctor covering all aspects of recognizing and treating chronic mercury toxicity.

Standards of Care for Amalgam Removal: A Guide for the Doctor and Patient, Paul J. Pavlik, DMD. This book addresses safety issues in regards to amalgam removal for the patient, doctor, staff, and environment. A beneficial guide for doctors to learn how to utilize the tools they already have, and/or additional tools to enhance existing protocol that creates a safer environment for themselves and their patients.

Health Realities Journal
Each issue, published quarterly, includes the latest research on a specific health topic from the Institute for Health Realities health model perspective. Every issue contains current information intended to educate and inform you on various health topics ranging from heart disease to cancer.

Health Realities in the News
This audio-tape series by Sam Queen and Special Guests includes discussions topics on: The Periodontal Disease vs. Heart Disease Connection / Antioxidant Update / Light, Cancer & Osteoporosis / Osteoporosis & Estrogen / American Heart Association / Biochemical Individuality / Nitric

Oxide / Pancreatic Function, Autism & pH control / Weight Control Part I & II / Metal Poisoning: Sources & Detection / and Challenge Tests to Assess Heavy Metal Burden.

FastTrack Program

This is the Free Radical Therapy Certification Program. Through 2 different phases a person can be certified in the Free Radical Therapy Health Model and learn how to incorporate this philosophy into their professional environment.

Supplements

For your convenience, we carry most of the products and supplements we write about. We have carefully chosen the supplements we use due to the success they have shown in our program. Many of the products we sell often cannot be found in general health stores.

Consultations

Our trained consultants are available for telephone and/or on-site consultations with you as well as with your doctor. For an information packet that includes our brochure, please call us at 719-598-4968.

For a full listing of our products and services, please visit our web site:

http://www.healthrealities.org

THE INSTITUTE FOR HEALTH REALITIES

Health Questionnaire
&
Description of Individual Health Plan Levels

On the following pages, you will find a health questionnaire that has been designed so that you can evaluate your answers and determine at which level the Institute for Health Realities consultation staff suggests you enter into our program and that would best suit your individual situation. The numbers you total up at the end of the questionnaire will provide you with a recommendation; however, we encourage you to begin where your comfort level and capabilities allow. After completing the questionnaire and totaling your answers, you may refer to the *Description of the Individual Health Plan Levels* section on the following pages. This will give a description of the levels so that you can then match your score. For further information on services that The Institute for Health Realities offers, please call our office at 719-598-4968.

INDIVIDUAL HEALTH PROFILE QUESTIONNAIRE*

This "Questionnaire" also available in larger print upon request -- call

Please complete all information & questions:

Name: _____

Address _____

City _____ State _____ ZIP _____

Sex ____ Race ____ Age ____ Height ____ Weight ____ (stripped)

Male (waist measurement) ____ inches Female (hip measurement) ____ inches

How did you hear about us?: _____

Today's Date: ___ / ___ / _____

Date of Birth: ___ / ___ / _____

Phone (H): _____ (W): _____

E-Mail: _____ Fax: _____

Blood Pressure: _____ / _____

Referred by: _____

Soc Sec # (optional): _____

INSTITUTE For HEALTH REALITIES

5245 Centennial Blvd., #100
Colorado Springs, CO 80919
Phone: (719) 598-4968
Fax: (719) 548-1785
Web: www.healthrealities.org

Yes No | Total up all numbers if you answered YES to any of the following questions, or if indicated otherwise

Yes	No		
	2	Are you under a physician's care now?	Discuss _____
	2	Have you ever been hospitalized or had major surgery?	Discuss _____
	3	Do you now or have you recently had an infection?	Discuss _____
	2	Are you taking any medications, antibiotics, pills, or drugs?	List _____
	1	Do you take food and/or vitamin supplements regularly?	Discuss _____
	1	Are you allergic to any medications, foods or supplements?	Discuss _____
	1	Are you on a diet or do you diet frequently? What kind?	Discuss _____

Do you have or have you had any of the following? (Please explain "Yes" answers on a separate sheet & enclose with questionnaire)

Yes/No		Yes/No		Yes/No		Yes/No	
3	Heart Disease/Arteriosclerosis	4	Cancer: Type _____	3	Rheumatoid Arthritis	2	Nervousness
2	High/Low Blood Pressure	4	Radiation Treatments	3	Osteoarthritis	2	Hallucinations
2	Chest Pain	4	Chemotherapy Treatments	3	Joint Pain/Swelling	3	Autism
3	High Cholesterol	4	Tumors/Growths	2	Bone Fractures	2	Antidepressants
3	High Triglyceride	2	Stomach/Intestinal Disorder	2	Gout	3	Psychiatric Care
3	Blood Disease	2	Bowel Disorder	3	Cortisone/Steroids	3	Suicidal/Depression
3	Stroke	4	Recent Weight Loss	3	Pain Meds: Type _____	3	Chronic/Migraine Headaches
3	Bruise Easily	2	Frequent Diarrhea	3	Chronic Fatigue Syndrome	2	Sinus Headaches
1	Varicose Veins	2	Ulcers	3	Fibromyalgia	3	Alzheimer's Disease
3	Anemia	2	Anorexia	2	Unexplained Fever	3	Dementia
3	Bleeding Disorders/Hemophilia	2	Bulimia	3	Swollen Glands/Nodes	3	Difficulty Concentrating
4	Leukemia	3	Diabetes: Type _____	3	Venereal Disease	3	Allergies (To Medicines)
3	Sickle Cell Disease	1	Hypoglycemia	3	AIDS	3	Allergies (To Food)
3	Osteoporosis	1	Excessive Thirst	3	HIV Positive	3	Allergies (To Pollen/Dust)
2	Breathing Problem	2	Night Sweats	2	Blood Transfusion	3	Hives/Rashes
3	Lung Disease	3	Liver Disease	3	Herpes	3	Excessive Perspiration
2	Snoring	3	Hepatitis	2	Bleeding Gums	3	Cold/Clammy Skin
2	Frequent Cough	3	Yellow Jaundice	3	Periodontal (Gum) Disease	3	Speech Disorders
1	Sinus Trouble	3	Kidney Problems	3	Cold Sores/Fever Blisters	3	Drug Addiction
3	Asthma	3	Renal Dialysis	3	Mouth Ulcers	3	ALS/Lou Gehrig's Disease
3	Emphysema	3	Gall Bladder Disease/Stones	3	Frequent Tooth Decay	3	Epilepsy/Seizures
3	Tuberculosis	3	Thyroid Disease	1	Bad Breath (Halitosis)	3	Convulsions
2	Hemorrhoids	3	Parathyroid Disease	1	Dentures	1	Vision Problems
2	Overweight	1	Currently Pregnant/Uncertain	2	Calculus (Tartar) on Teeth	3	Glaucoma
2	Underweight	1	Nursing	2	Fainting/Dizziness	1	Ear Problems
3	Iron Overload (Hemochromatosis)	2	Birth Control Pills	2	TMJ/Grinding Problems	1	Nose Problems
2	Prostate Problems	2	Numbness	2	Sleep Disorders		Other _____

____ Subtotal Column   ____ Subtotal Column   ____ Subtotal Column   ____ Subtotal Column

If any "blood" relatives have had any of the above, please discuss: _____

Do you consider your general health to be? Excellent ____ 1 Good ____ 2 Fair ____ 3 Poor ____ 4

What is your outlook on life in general? Excellent ____ 1 Good ____ 2 Fair ____ 3 Poor ____ 4

What health concerns, symptoms, complaints, and/or goals would you like to have discussed (list up to three):

A _____

B _____

C _____

If more space is needed, please add additional information to an attached page(s) | Sub-total (add up all numbers on this page) ____ |

General Questions:

| Total up all numbers if you answered "Yes" to any of the following questions, or if indicated otherwise |

Do you fall asleep easily & sleep soundly?
- 2 □ No
- 0 □ Yes

What time do you go to bed? ____ What time do you awaken? ____
Do you take anything to help you sleep? ____
Explain _____

Do you breath air that is of good quality?
- 4 □ No — Explain _____
- 0 □ Yes

Do you live in a healthy environment?   Home ___   Apartment ___   Mobile Home ___   Condominium/Townhome ___   Other ___
- 4 □ No
- 0 □ Yes — Explain _____

Do you work in a healthy environment?
- 4 □ No
- 0 □ Yes — Explain _____

Are you now or were you ever exposed to substances that could endanger health (e.g., lead, mercury, chemicals, dusts, fumes, gases, etc.)?
- 0 □ No
- 3 □ Yes — Explain _____

Do you have/had "silver" fillings?
- 0 □ No
- 3 □ Yes If "Yes", how many? ___

Are your teeth sensitive to hot, cold, sweets, pressure?
- 0 □ No
- 3 □ Yes

Do you have any teeth with root canal fillings?
- 2 □ Yes
- 0 □ No

Do you have a metallic taste?
- 0 □ No
- 3 □ Yes

Does your mouth &/or lips feel cracked, dry, or sore?
- 0 □ No
- 2 □ Yes

What is your source of drinking water?
- 0 □ Filtered
- 1 □ Bottled
- 2 □ Municipal
- 3 □ Well

Is your daily water intake adequate?
- 3 □ No
- 0 □ Yes

(recommend at least 1/2 ounce per pound of body weight)
(e.g., if you weigh 140 pounds, then 70 ounces of water is a recommended minimum intake)

What else do you drink? *Enter times/day, week in the blocks*

	Day	Week		Day	Week		Day	Week
Soda/Pop	3		Tea (regular)	1		Alcohol		
Orange Juice	1		Tea (herbal)	1		Red Wine	1	
Other Juices	1		Coffee (regular)	3		White Wine	2	
Milk	1		Coffee (decaf)	3		Beer	2	
Soy Milk	1		Other ____			Hard Liquor	3	

Do you have an alcohol problem?
- 0 □ No
- 3 □ Yes — Explain _____

Do you maintain a healthy diet (i.e., protein, fresh fruits, grains, vegetables, & cultured dairy)?
- 3 □ No
- 0 □ Yes — Explain _____

Do you regularly eat: (check "Yes" box if you do)
- 0 □ Yes Breakfast? — Sample of typical breakfast _____ Discuss_____
- 0 □ Yes Lunch? — Sample of typical lunch _____ Discuss_____
- 0 □ Yes Dinner? — Sample of typical dinner _____ Discuss_____
- 1 □ Yes Snack before bedtime? — Sample of typical snack _____ Discuss_____
- 3 □ Yes Processes/refined carbohydrates (e.g., pasta, white bread, potatoes, snacks, desserts, sugar, candy, etc.)?
  List which carbohydrates, how often, and how much _____
- 2 □ Yes Are you allergic to any foods? — Explain: _____
- 1 □ Yes Do you have a problem with gas &/or belching? — Explain: _____
- 2 □ Yes Do any foods cause you discomfort? — Explain: _____

How many times do you urinate each day? ___ (if 3 or less, score 3; if 7 or more, score 2; otherwise, score 0)
- 2 □ Yes Does it burn when you urinate?
- 2 □ Yes Do you get up at night to urinate?
- 2 □ Yes Do you have a urinary tract infection?

Do you have at least 2 bowel movements per day?
- 3 □ No If "No". How many times/day ____
- 0 □ Yes — Explain _____

What color is your bowel movement?
- Brown 0 □   3 Yellow or red
- Green 2 □   4 Black
- 1 □ Soft
- 0 □ Medium
- 1 □ Hard

Do you smoke or use tobacco?
- 0 □ No
- 3 □ Yes How many years? ____

Tobacco Source	Frequency per day	Tobacco Source	Frequency per day
□ Cigarettes	3	□ Chewing Tobacco	3
□ Cigars	3	□ Second Hand Exposure	2
□ Pipe	3		

Do you feel you have a drug habit?
- 0 □ No
- 3 □ Yes — Explain _____ How many years? ____

Do you exercise or engage in physical activity (totaling at least 20 minutes 5 days of the week)?
- 2 □ No
- 0 □ Yes

Type	Duration	Times/Week	Type	Duration	Times/Week
Aerobic			Weight Trng		
Walking			Stretching		
Running			Other		
Bicycle					
Nordic Track					
Rowing Machine					
Other					

Add up the totals, then read the section **"Individual Health Plan Levels"** to see how your health scores match up to IHR's recommendations.

Subtotals	
First Page ____	
Second Page ____	**My Total Score** ____
TOTAL ____	

IHR recommends that you make a copy of all information that you send to IHR for your records.

Signature: _____

Property of: INSTITUTE FOR HEALTH REALITIES

Mail to: 5245 Centennial Blvd., #100
Colorado Springs, CO 80919
Phone: (719) 598-4968
Fax: (719) 548-1785
Web: www.healthrealities.org

*Confidentiality Statement
The Institute for Health Realities and its constituents guarantees that no information supplied by the client will be given to any other individual, organization, doctor, or healthcare facility without the expressed written consent of the client.

Description of Individual Health Plan Levels

LEVEL 1
Introductory Profile
Score: No value above 2 (check boxes on pg. 1) for any
category and/or a total score of 79 or less

We recommend this level if you have no known
health problems, feel relatively healthy and have not
had any serious disease or illness. This is the place to
start if you want to begin plans to maintain your
health throughout your life. At this level there is no
blood or urine chemistry done, but through our
extensive evaluation of your health questionnaire you
will find this to be an economical, yet informative
place to start.

Your package will include:

- An IHR consultant's evaluation of your health
  questionnaire
- A written report containing health and lifestyle
  recommendations
- An audio-taped report for you

LEVEL 2
Comprehensive QP-II Profile
Score: No value above 2 (check boxes on pg.1) for any
category and/or a total score of 80 to 99

This level includes the key blood chemistries that
insurance companies would review to evaluate your
eligibility for a life insurance plan. These chemistries
are intended to identify your susceptibility to future
life-threatening diseases. If you are concerned with
whether or not you are at risk for any life-threatening

diseases, or if you are curious how smoking, drugs, or alcohol could be affecting your life, this is the level we would suggest.

Your package will include:

- An IHR consultant's evaluation of your chemistries and health questionnaire
- A written report containing health and lifestyle recommendations
- An audio-taped report for you

LEVEL 3
General Health Profile
Score: No value above 3 (check boxes on pg. 1) for any category and/or a total score of 100 or more

This level provides the most comprehensive chemistry-based approach for non-cancer clients. If you already have a known disease condition, are taking multiple prescription drugs, have high blood pressure, suffer from repeat infections or a combination of symptoms (e.g., heart disease, periodontal disease, etc.), we would suggest you begin at this level. This extensive blood chemistry allows for an overall approach to your health and includes a follow-up session to check your success.

Your package will include:

- An IHR consultant's evaluation of your chemistries and health questionnaire
- A phone or on-site consultation
- A written report containing health and lifestyle recommendations
- An audio-taped report for you
- Discounts on follow-up chemistries and consultations

LEVEL 4
Cancer Profile
Score: No value of 4 (on page 1) in any category

If you have been diagnosed with cancer, are at high risk for cancer (e.g., family history, exposure to toxins), or are concerned about cancer risk, this is the level for you. It includes all of Level 3 as well as specific chemistries designed to understand the basis of cancer and how best to combat it. This level utilizes the maximum effort to rebuild your immune system whether or not you have chosen to undergo chemotherapy, radiation, or surgery. This level is excellent in monitoring your progress.

Your package will include:

- An IHR consultant's evaluation of your chemistries and health questionnaire
- A phone or on-site consultation
- A written report containing health and lifestyle recommendations
- An audio-taped report for you
- Discounts on follow-up chemistries and consultations

ABOUT THE AUTHORS

H.L."Sam" Queen, M.A., C.N.S., D.Sc. (Hon.), is the Founder and Director of Research & Development at the Institute for Health Realities. He has over 40 years as a health care educator and investigative medical writer in the health care field. Early in his career, Sam was poisoned by mercury while working in a clinical laboratory. As a result, he authored the first medical reference book on Chronic Mercury Toxicity and has become an authority on what it takes to battle this disease and WIN.

Betty A. Queen, B.S. has a Bachelor of Science degree in Foods & Nutrition. Together, she and Sam are totally committed to helping doctors and their patients solve the problems associated with mercury toxicity.